i don't know what **i** want

but i want to be happy

DISCARD

i don't know what **i** want

but i want to be happy

Kimberly Kirberger

Co-author of Chicken Soup for the Teenage Soul and

Jesse Kirberger

HCI TEENS™

Health Communications, Inc.
Deerfield Beach, Florida

www.hcibooks.com

Permissions

"Standing Alone" by Kimberly Kirberger and Hanna Szabo. Printed with permission.

"I Love What I Do" by Alexander Witt. Printed with permission.

"A Fun Chase" by Hana Szabo. Printed with permission.

"A Creative Outlet" by Lancelot Dyke. Printed with permission.

"All I Want Is a Smile" by Lia Gay. Printed with permission.

"My Daily Pursuit of Happiness" by Chrissy Blumenthal. Printed with permission.

"Remember to Remember" by Lia Gay. Printed with permission.

"Get Organized" by Hana Szabo. Printed with permission.

"Every Day Something New" by Cody Demory. Printed with permission.

"I've Been Given" by Kristen Foster. Printed with permission.

"Picking Up the Pieces" by Emily Starr. Printed with permission.

"The Journey" by Zan Gaudisio. Printed with permission.

Library of Congress Cataloging-in-Publication Data

Kirberger, Kimberly.
   I don't know what I want / Kimberly and Jesse Kirberger.
      p. cm.
    ISBN-13: 978-0-7573-0674-7
    ISBN-10: 0-7573-0674-8
    1. Happiness.   2. Conduct of life.   I. Kirberger, Jesse.   II. Title.
B187.H3K56 2009
158—dc22

2009012229

Publisher: Health Communications, Inc.
      3201 S.W. 15th Street
      Deerfield Beach, FL 33442–8190

Cover design by Larissa Hise Henoch
Interior design and formatting by Lawna Patterson Oldfield

The first time our needs and our wants are fulfilled is seconds after we are born into this otherwise cold and confusing world. For most of us, it is our mothers who give us our first taste of happiness. They feed our hunger, keep us warm, and show us love.

That's why it is with the deepest gratitude that we dedicate this book to all mothers for the happiness they bestow upon our world.

Some very special mothers who have earned our deepest love and gratitude are Ellen Angelis, Jody Kirberger, Dorothy Mayfield, Helga Witt, and Linda Cross.

CONTENTS

Contents

Contents

Contents

FOREWORD

I have known Kimberly for a number of years and find her commitment to helping teenagers incredibly powerful. In this latest book, coauthored with her son, Jesse, she continues with this intention.

She takes some of the very sophisticated concepts from existentialism, cognitive psychotherapy, and metaphysics, and expresses them magically and creatively in a way that the teenage mind (as well as most adult minds) can understand, accept, and use to become happy. And since "happy" is our underlying motivation and number one desire, I think she has chosen the best possible subject to deliver to teens in the way that only she can do.

This book is for those who are turned off by the latest psychobabble and just want someone to talk straight and not try to talk "hip." Kimberly and Jesse only want their readers to understand and benefit from their offerings and it shows, with Jesse's witty and wise paragraphs sprinkled throughout. Without question, this is my favorite one of her books yet.

As a clinical psychologist, my professional advice to you is this: read this book! Feel free to read it cover to cover, front to back, or back to front. Read it from the middle to the end. Or just pick a random page and read it. However you read it, I'm strongly urging you to just read it. And make yourself happy!

—M. Adam Sheck, Psy.D.

CLICHÉ OR GOOD ADVICE?

Jesse

MUCH OF THE ADVICE GIVEN in self-help or advice books can sometimes be shrugged off as a bunch of meaningless clichés. I don't doubt that some of you will feel that way about some of the advice in this book.

You can only take something getting drilled into your head so many times before you begin to tune it out. This is something you will have to overcome in order to fully commit to getting happy. Why do you think certain phrases become clichés in the first place? I figure it's because enough people agreed that they were good advice or at least held a lot of truth. Then, whenever these people would meet someone who might benefit from knowing that "all is fair in love and war" or to "never look a gift horse in the mouth," they would let them know, until everyone was saying it. I don't necessarily support the fine folks who discovered that there is, indeed, more than one way to skin a cat, but I wouldn't argue the truth in that statement.

So if you encounter anything that may seem like a cliché along the way, be open to treating it as good advice, as if you are hearing for the first time. Don't be so quick to kick it to the curb or to write it off as just another cliché.

The Search

When we are born and take our first breath, we separate from our mother and from perfect happiness for the first time. We cry because we are suddenly cast into a world where we feel things like coldness, heat, hunger, and thirst; thus, **we feel UNCOMFORTABLE**.

Someone—usually our mother—feeds us, holds us, loves us, and releases us from our discomfort. It is one of our earliest experiences of happiness in this new and frightening world. When our needs have been met, we relax and are able to rest peacefully. . . .

Until . . .

We find ourselves uncomfortable again. This time, we want more than food. We want to be dry, we want a comfortable bed, and we want someone to hold us and sing us to sleep. As time goes by, the list grows longer. As we expand our experience of the world around us, we also expand our list of wants and needs. At some point, we lose touch with what it is we want and what it is that we need. These feelings of discomfort and emptiness become so commonplace that they don't stand out anymore. Most of us begin to accept the yearning and emptiness as just a normal part of being human.

Since we can't find that perfect peace we once felt on the inside, we begin seeking distraction from our yearning on the outside: something, anything, that will hold our attention well enough to keep us from feeling the emptiness. We become so good at distracting ourselves from the pain that we eventually forget that's what we're doing. Before long, we start to feel the pain we have so cleverly hidden from ourselves, and we believe someone else must be causing it. It can't be *our* pain because we were fine until so and so came along and said this and that. We become quite skilled at placing the blame for our different kinds of pain on other people. We become so skilled that we forget the pain started inside of us.

From this point, there are two potential directions we can go with our lives and how we pursue what we want and need:

- Continue our lives, never noticing that we aren't happy and therefore not really ever asking **what we want** or **what we need** to be **HAPPY**.

- Intuitively knowing something is missing, we dedicate ourselves to finding what it is. We happily assume the responsibility for returning ourselves to the **peaceful** and **joyful** person we once were.

It's important to begin thinking about what we want our lives to look like. Up until this point, many of us thought life was something that just happened to us. But once we begin to see how much our thoughts, intentions, and actions play into the outcome of our day, as well as how we feel about our lives in general, it is easy for us to reassume responsibility and participate.

We realize it is up to us to decide what kind of life we want, to **set goals**, and then do what we need to do to achieve them.

What Do You Want?

magine one day you wake up to find a genie sitting at the foot of your bed. Pulling out a large scroll from her bag, she proclaims, "Today you will have to decide what you want from life and whatever you decide will become a reality." She unfurls the scroll and says, "Before we begin, some guidelines. . . .

"First, you will only be allowed three minutes to decide what you want. All of your answers will be final. I will not ask, 'Is that your final answer?' There will be no take backs, no matter what.

"Second, remember this is your life, not your parent's, or

your friend's, or anyone else's. Do not allow your answers to be influenced by what anyone else would want for you.

"Third, your requests will be taken literally. Think them through carefully. No assumptions will be made; what you ask for is what you will get.

"And last, you will forget that this ever happened immediately after answering."

What would be going through your head? Would you wish you had more time? Would you be sure about your answers?

Ready? Set. Go!

This is what some teens had to say when we asked what they wanted:

"I WANT TO BE HAPPY
MOST OF ALL, NO MATTER
WHAT I DO."
—ZACK RODRIGUEZ

"I WANT SOMEONE TO HOLD ME AND
MAKE ME FEEL IMPORTANT."
—CHRISTIAN ANGLELO

"I WANT TO GET A GOOD EDUCATION AND AN
OPPORTUNITY TO APPRENTICE WITH SOMEONE
WHO IS SUCCESSFUL IN WEB DESIGN."
—TOM MAXWELL

"I WANT TO BE WHO I WANT TO BE, AND
IF THAT CHANGES, SO BE IT."

—DANIEL GERENA

"I WISH I HAD MORE PASSION."

—JENNY DUARTE

"I WANT TO HAVE A RELATIONSHIP
IN WHICH I CAN SHARE INTIMACY WITH
SOMEONE AND STILL BE GOOFY AND
CLUMSY AROUND THEM."

—DANIEL GERENA

"I WANT TO BE A PART OF THE AMERICAN
RED CROSS . . . TO HELP PEOPLE."

—SARAH SALARKIA

Beware of Whatever

Many times, when we asked teens certain questions
like "What do you want?" and "How would you
change?" we were given the shoulder-shrug answer "Whatever."
We were aware of some sadness, some anger, and most of all
a loss of hope. It was as if they were saying, "Why bother
wanting what you aren't going to get?" These teens clearly
needed to forgive themselves and others, and trust life once
more. Many people don't know what they want (at least not
all the time), and teens, in particular, spend most of their time
wondering what's going to make them happy.

Whatever you do, do not give up trying to find the things that inspire you, the work that you love, and the kind of relationships you insist on having. If you don't take the time to figure out exactly what you want, who you want to be, who you want to be with, and what you want to do with your life, then you are giving away your power to the "whatever" tribe.

This is the tribe of people who just go from day to day without ever thinking about what they want to do, what they want to learn about and experience, and what they want to strive for. Most of their decisions and their reactions are dealt with by using one word: *whatever*. This isn't necessarily the best way to create a happy and fulfilling life. Although there's nothing wrong with being relaxed every now and then, relaxation can't be truly enjoyed without first putting some good hard work on the same menu.

However, if you stand by "whatever," it would take something like a mircale to end up living the life that makes you happy. More often than not, people who make no choices, who do not declare their goals, or who have no identity by which they define themselves are the people who most often end up the victims. A common victim declaration goes like this:

"Why is this happening to me? I didn't ask for this. I didn't do anything."

Exactly!

Instead of evaluating their wants and needs, and from that point, establishing plans and goals, they just sat back and said, "Whatever."

And "whatever" was what they got.

We are by no means saying that we are completely capable of controlling our lives. Things are changing all the time: some good changes, some not so good. We control only a portion of what happens. But if we are clear about what we want and are not afraid to ask for it, we can go to the front of the line. For example, if you think a warm, sunny climate will make you happy, and you simply get in your car and drive around, the odds of finding such a place are not very good. But, if you have an actual warm and sunny place in mind and you plan and map out your trip, your odds of arriving there have greatly increased. It's that simple.

WE DO NOT HAVE COMPLETE CONTROL
OVER WHAT HAPPENS, BUT WE DO HAVE
COMPLETE CONTROL OVER
HOW WE REACT TO WHAT HAPPENS.

Nothing Good or Bad

My friend Zack often reminds me of the story of a very affluent, hard-working couple, who had only one son. They made him their world and had great expectations for him. At six-eight, he had become the star basketball player of his state, and his team had once again made it to the finals. If they won this one it would be his third and final championship in his home state before heading off to Notre Dame.

At a party the night before the finals, he was a bit drunk, and while rough housing with his buddies, he broke his arm. He and his family were despondent and the whole town was talking about how tragic it was. He was torn up with guilt. He was eliminated from the game because of his broken arm but also for drinking. He was banned from attending the finals and sitting with his team. He wrote in his journal that this was, by far, the worst thing that had ever happened to him.

The 10 o'clock news had another tragedy to report. The bus carrying the team had been in a terrible accident. . . . There were no survivors.

THE VICTIM

Jesse

IT'S VERY EASY TO TAKE the position of feeling sorry for yourself when something really crappy is happening in your life—the whole "woe is me" mindset. I'm sure you've experienced it; it seems every single person on Earth has. Without realizing it, you take the position of the victim and, in doing so, begin to take all the power away from yourself. It's like giving a weapon to someone who's trying to jack your wallet. Self-esteem, energy, and time are all spent on thinking about how the whole world is against you and that nothing will ever work out. There's no way to feel happy as a victim; it will only lead to more problems as it is a self-perpetuating state of mind.

All the miserable stuff in life is supposed to make you stronger, right? Well, let it! Let those situations inspire you! Let them inspire you to work your butt off to do whatever you can to prevent them in the future. Take charge of the hard times, and you will be building your strength and confidence to help in future battles.

The following is a list of what can be done to insure our happiness:

learn from and let go of our past,
get control over our feelings,
and remember how strong we really are.

Face each new moment
with innocence and an open mind
to have a positive attitude.

Find joy in
the simple things,
remembering that everything
is just a matter of perspective.

Be patient, honest, compassionate
and open to self-examination.
Be clear about what is going on
so you can choose what's right for you.

No matter what
stay true to yourself.
Don't ever give yourself away.
Keep your power.

Don't worry about what other people think.
Don't be the victim,
and remember the value that comes with
taking responsibility.

Stay busy, work hard, and do the right thing,
Avoid judgments and expectations.
Be a good friend to others and to yourself.

Don't take things personally,
don't take yourself too seriously,
and never lose your sense of humor.

Get Real

We work so hard to present ourselves to others as if we always have it together. We protect our pride and go to great lengths to make sure our flaws and failures are never seen. This is a defective plan because we rarely fool other people, and more important, our unique flaws are what make us who we are.

If we instead let ourselves be who we are with all our good and bad, and if we can learn to love and laugh at ourselves for being wonderfully human, then we can know true self-love and acceptance. Once we experience being loved for the real person we are—with the good, the bad, and the ugly—we won't ever want to be loved any other way.

"NOTHING IS REALLY GOOD OR BAD
EXCEPT OUR THINKING MAKES IT SO.
IT'S ALL PART OF THE DANCE OF LIFE.
SO DANCE, AND LAUGH, AND LET IT GO."

—KIMBERLY KIRBERGER

Do you take responsibility for yourself? _____

_____

_____

_____

What does that mean to you? _____

_____

_____

_____

_____

_____

_____

_____

_____

Write about a time you betrayed yourself. _____

_____

_____

_____

_____

_____

_____

_____

Write about a time you settled for less than your heart's desire. _____

_____

_____

_____

_____

_____

_____

_____

_____

Do you deserve to be treated with love and kindness?

_____

_____

_____

_____

_____

Do you deserve to be treated with respect?

_____

_____

_____

_____

_____

"STANDING ALONE"

by Kimberly Kirberger
and Hanna Szabo

I woke up one day

and looked in the mirror

to see a very

unhappy person

looking back at me

My life had fallen apart and

I was too busy to

realize it

Now I'm standing alone

at the crossroads

alone and too scared to make changes

too comfortable to care

The absence of pain

is not the same as happiness

It only allows me

to forget

how far from happy I am

So far from it that I'm scared

I won't know how to get back

I want to be happy

I just have to figure out

what my happy is

so, when I am there I will know for sure

that it is mine and not somebody else's.

●

"WHAT LIES BEHIND US
AND WHAT LIES AHEAD OF US ARE
TINY MATTERS COMPARED TO
WHAT LIVES WITHIN US."

—ATTRIBUTION UNKNOWN

"HAPPINESS IS NOT THE
SATISFACTION OF WHATEVER
IRRATIONAL WISHES YOU MIGHT BLINDLY
ATTEMPT TO INDULGE. HAPPINESS IS A
STATE OF NON-CONTRADICTORY JOY—
A JOY WITHOUT PENALTY OR GUILT. . . .
HAPPINESS IS POSSIBLE ONLY TO
A RATIONAL MAN, THE MAN WHO DESIRES
NOTHING BUT RATIONAL GOALS,
SEEKS NOTHING BUT RATIONAL VALUES,
AND FINDS HIS JOY IN NOTHING
BUT RATIONAL ACTIONS. . . . THERE ARE
NO VICTIMS AND NO CONFLICTS OF
INTEREST AMONG RATIONAL MEN,
MEN WHO DO NOT DESIRE
THE UNEARNED. . . . "

—AYN RAND

Self-Acceptance

If you are not happy, you must begin to do what is necessary by first accepting and then loving yourself. It isn't always something we put on our to-do list, but why not start? Instead of doing things to make others like us more, why not spend that time doing what will make us like ourselves more?

First we need to **focus our energy** on:

Accepting

Forgiving

Liking

Loving

And being gentle with ourselves

What could be better for us then to be able to love and nurture ourselves the same way and with the same tenderness that a mother does her newborn baby?

What could be better then to be our own best friend, our favorite companion, the one for whom we care the most?

In doing so, we would naturally be:

Happier

More secure

Confident

Attractive

Positive

At ease

We need to spend less time thinking about what others might think or wondering if it is okay to be selfish. Stop paying all your attention to what other people are doing with their lives. When we spend that time thinking about ourselves, we get to know ourselves better. The better we know ourselves, the better we will be at knowing what is going to make us happy. The more we know about what we need, the easier it will be to get it. If you know what makes you feel loved, it will be easier to love yourself.

We are our best when:

We know who we are.

We know what we want.

We know, that for us, we are doing the

right thing.

"I Love What I Do"

Alexander Witt

When I think about how much I love what I do, I also realize that not everyone loves what they do. It seems those of us who love what we do, love it because we've always done it for ourselves and no one else. We do it because it is **what we want to do**.

It's hard to share with other people what that is like. I can show them pictures, and we can talk about things that happened, but to get up every day and be excited to go do my job, it's hard to describe.

However, I love this journey that I'm on and that my work is constantly challenging, changing, and pushing me to go further—ultimately, to do better, because it's what I want to do.

"THE HAPPIEST PEOPLE
SPEND THE LEAST TIME ALONE.
THEY PURSUE PERSONAL GROWTH
AND INTIMACY; THEY JUDGE THEMSELVES
BY THEIR OWN YARDSTICKS,
NEVER AGAINST WHAT
OTHERS DO OR HAVE."

—MARILYN ELIAS

A Good Friend . . .

A good friend understands that time spent together is the best way to show our love and tell a friend that we **truly care** about them.

Know your friends have needs, and even if you can't fulfill them, it really helps for them to know you empathize. It's important for them to feel they have every right to ask for what they need.

Many times when a friend can't say yes to a need I have, I believe it's because she doesn't want to, but when the tables are turned, I know I agonize over not being able to give my friend what she needs.

It's the same with feelings. Let your friends know you understand before giving them advice. Advice on its own can sometimes sound like you are saying they did something wrong. Honesty is always the right answer. Admitting you're wrong isn't the same as admitting you've lost.

The strong ones are the ones who can admit when they make a mistake.

"HAPPINESS COMES OF
THE CAPACITY TO FEEL DEEPLY,
TO ENJOY SIMPLY, TO THINK FREELY,
TO RISK LIFE, TO BE
NEEDED."
—STORM JAMESON

How to Have a
Positive Personality

- **Understand** the needs of other people.

- Always be **aware** of other people's **feelings** and be a good listener.

- Make your conversations and environment **negative-free** zones.

- **Don't encourage** gossip.

- Happiness **spreads**. When you are happy, others feel safe around you.

- Be **honest** with yourself and others.

- Be **kind**. Treat people with warmth and respect.

- Be accountable for your behavior. If you can't help, at least **do no harm**.

- **Be** fair.

- Focus on the **good** in people. Everyone has out-standing qualities, and it's up to you **to find** them.

DID YOU KNOW?
The greatest thing we
can do for those we love is to
be happy, and the worst thing
we can do for those we love is
to be unhappy. So, if you
love somebody,
be happy!

Allow Yourself to Laugh

Don't be afraid to laugh and find humor in the simplest of things. Sometimes, it is a good thing to "dance like no one is watching" even when everyone is. Now that's something to laugh about!

"TO FILL THE HOUR—THAT IS HAPPINESS."

—RALPH WALDO EMERSON

I love being able to make a joke

when everyone expects the opposite.

Humor's the best gift.

Humor can cure the worst disease

And the meanest eyes,

The most ignorant mind

And the saddest soul.

It only needs just a tiny crack

where It can slip through

the hardened heart

And let a little bit of

lightheartedness do its thing.

–Kim Kirberger

Get Along With Others

'll always remember the place on my grade-school
report card that read **"Plays well with others."** In that
section, I would always get the maximum amount of stars. It
has always been very important to me what others think about
me.

In fact, one of my biggest fears was being talked badly
about behind my back. The idea of friends betraying me,
laughing at me, and no longer wanting to have anything to
do with me was, without a doubt, the absolute worst thing
imaginable. It existed in my mind as such a horrible

possibility that I worked overtime to ensure it wouldn't happen to me.

There came a point, though, when I realized I couldn't control how people felt about me, no matter how hard I tried. People are going to get angry, have negative feelings, assume things, and so on—and there was nothing I could do about it. More often than not, if someone is mean to us, it's because they aren't feeling so great about themselves. And while you're so worried about what they're thinking and saying, they, too, are worried about what someone else is thinking or saying about them. Trying to figure out what other people are thinking or trying to control how others think of you is a waste of time.

Sometimes, it pays to just ask and talk it out.

I always make sure that anyone I care for and love is aware of the importance to me of talking things through. If a friendship becomes a source of pain or one person changes and the other doesn't, it is often a good idea to part ways. The bottom line is that no matter what happens,

both people should have the chance to hear and talk about it.

Everyone deserves to have **closure** and to **heal**.

"JUST BE ME"

By Kimberly Kirberger

I won't try so hard

to be what I think they want me to be

if who I am isn't fine

and I'm not their cup of tea

this time I'll remember

if they don't like

who they see

it's not going to kill me.

HEDONISTIC BY NATURE

Jesse

IT'S NOT SURPRISING THAT WHEN most people picture self-discipline, they don't necessarily jump up and down with excitement. After all, finishing an entire container of Ben & Jerry's sounds much more pleasurable than just having a taste.

There's nothing wrong with being a little intimidated by the idea of self-discipline. Humans are hedonistic creatures by nature. If you told most of the people on MTV's annual show *Spring Break* that their overindulgence wasn't going to make them truly happy, they'd probably throw a fistful of sand in your face.

Many of us are under the impression that shunning all responsibilities and not having to work will make us happy, when in reality this couldn't be further from the truth. Hedonism will never lead to happiness. Sound ridiculous? Why wouldn't partying all the time make us happy?

The answer makes more sense than you think. When we go for long periods of time without doing anything productive (for example, setting and reaching goals, getting in a hard day's work, or having a hobby to be passionate about), we begin to feel useless. It's a sneaky feeling whose presence may be totally subconscious, but it can make us feel depressed and lead to self-loathing.

I used to work at a restaurant on Venice Beach almost every day. It was a pretty hectic job, as Venice Beach generally plays host to swarms of people, most of whom I wouldn't necessarily tag as sweethearts. After months of being yelled at by customers who refused to be satisfied, having mustard spilled all over me, and fending off pigeons that were trying to make Jackson Pollock paintings in my hair, I quit the job.

For the next few weeks, I remember trying to spend every day doing as little possible. When I wasn't with friends, I would usually just lie on the couch and watch TV. After a while, I started feeling anxious and depressed most of the time, which didn't make any sense to me. I didn't have to get up for work every day, and I could do whatever I wanted. So why wasn't I happy?

I had lost a big source of self-discipline, without which I was beginning to get lazy. I was losing the sense of accomplishment that I had felt after a day of hard work and, in doing so, had depleted myself of a necessary ingredient for my happiness.

"ACTION MAY NOT
ALWAYS BRING HAPPINESS, BUT
THERE IS NO HAPPINESS
WITHOUT ACTION."
—BENJAMIN DISRAELI

DID YOU KNOW?

Happiness has been
linked to meaningful
relationships. People who are
happy are usually supported
by close relationships
with friends, relatives,
and coworkers.

The Happy Walk

Get some friends together and go for a walk in a place where you'll see and be seen by lots of people. You could go to the mall or to a park on a warm day. For the entire walk, your job will be to look and act as if you just won the lottery or got tickets to your favorite band's concert. Watch how other people **respond** to your happiness.

WHEN I ASKED MY FRIENDS

Jesse

WHEN I ASKED MY FRIENDS to give me some quotes
or paragraphs about happiness for this book, I noticed that
many of the contributions had to do with not being happy.
The rest were along the lines of "Who's letting you write
a book?"

It's strange that a culture so obsessed with being happy
would only share quotes like "It's impossible to be happy
all the time" and "Everyone is a little depressed." Of course
you can't be happy all of the time! If you were, you'd
probably creep everybody out. The point is, you'll never
be happy if you think about it so negatively.

Try adopting a mantra like *I can be happy most of the time*. While a mantra may seem completely corny, it has been shown in several psychological studies that your mood can change just by reading (or in this case saying) positive or negative statements. Start to replace all the negative thoughts and comments that you have about happiness with positive ones.

Make sure to keep your statements believable or you may stop trusting yourself, and that would take a whole different book to address. Instead of *I will reach complete happiness tomorrow,* think *It may take a little time, but I will become a happy person.* You will find that your mood will get better and better the more you start using—and believing—these positive statements.

AVOID NEGATIVE SELF-TALK

magine you had a magical power that turned your thoughts into reality. It's kind of a scary concept since most of us think negative thoughts most of the time. When it comes to ourselves, we are more inclined to think, *I'm not beautiful (or handsome), I hate my body, I'm a loser, I'm not popular, I'm stupid,* and so on.

One of the first things we have to do is begin thinking of ourselves in positive terms. We need to spend less time thinking about what's inside us. We need to ask ourselves questions that will increase our self-acceptance. Listen and pay attention to your thoughts. Ask yourself, "Is there a positive way for me to think about this?"

Practice thinking in a positive way until it becomes a habit. For example, *I'll never get this finished by the end of the day!* could become *I will do my best to get most of this finished by the end of the day.*

WAKE UP

Jesse

WHAT DO YOU USUALLY THINK about when you wake up in the morning? If you're like most people, you probably think about all the miserable chores that you have to get done that day. It's rare that anyone wakes up with an optimistic attitude and thoughts of how great the day is going to be. That's understandable, since most people awaken to a parent shouting that it's time to get up, a sibling poking their foreheads, or a horrible alarm clock screaming at them to get ready for school.

Believe me, I know that waking up is no fun. I usually open my eyes to my cat's butt positioned right near my face while she drinks from the cup next to my bed. There's nothing better.

These negative morning feelings and thoughts may seem harmless because they come so naturally, but they can actually alter the way your day unfolds. The next time you wake up, pretend any thoughts you have about the upcoming day will come true, exactly as you imagine. If you think about how stressful your day is going to be, you'll lose your wallet, be late for school, and trip and fall in some dog poop on the way home. You get the idea.

Happiness is a decision. It is up to you.
Do you want to be happy?
Well then, be happy!

"A Fun Chase"

Hana Szabo

Happiness has always been a fun chase for me. I feel like it's right within my reach, but I have not fully caught up to it just yet. It's a little butterfly that I can't wait to get my hands on. I long to be happy, and I think I am close. The decisions I make now will determine how my life turns out—what kind of an adult I'll be. And as anxious as I am to find out who I'll become, I'm not in any hurry. I am just enjoying the ride. I love the ride. I love getting to know myself. The higher I set my goals, the more satisfying it will be to achieve them. And I'm not afraid to make mistakes, to slip up on the way. **Why?** Because it is all part of the process.

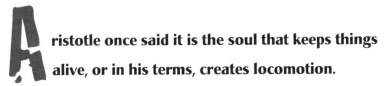

"A Creative Outlet"

Lancelot Dyke

Aristotle once said it is the soul that keeps things alive, or in his terms, creates locomotion. It is the soul that fuels our actions, ideas, and every other mechanism that drives us to live. Sadness dehydrates the soul. When anguish leaks in, it stiffens everything else up! All of a sudden it becomes harder to raise your head high, walk at a quick pace, and more than anything, keep your eyes bright.

For me, it's really important to have a creative outlet so whenever sadness does creep in it has a quick exit route.

It's surprising to me how quickly negative energy can be turned into positive energy simply by being aware of the negative and then wanting to change it. This works even better if we have **tried-and-true techniques** for doing so.

But don't get stuck with one or two ways; it is also important to try new things and add the ones that work into your repertoire—like painting, for example. If you feel intoxicated with despondency (whatever the cause may be), picking up a paintbrush and painting to your taste and to the best of your ability all of a sudden becomes a reflection of what's going on inside of you!

There is a major sense of accomplishment and aesthetic pleasure in finding a way to release all of one's negative energy.

I personally have found creativity works for me. One of my creative outlets is playing music. I own a few ukuleles, and because of their toothsome sound, I always find a way to rescue my soul whenever I feel sad. Sometimes I'll sit for hours, strumming and humming every emotion I have inside out, and once it's out there, it's my emotion to control and appreciate. That's the **beauty** of **creative outlets**.

DID YOU KNOW?

Creativity is a good outlet
for expressing your feelings.
Whatever craft you choose—painting
or drawing, writing, sculpting,
sewing, woodworking, and so on—
put your energy into the project and
create something that makes
you happy just because you
created it. It doesn't have to
be a masterpiece!

"CREATIVITY IS ALLOWING YOURSELF
TO MAKE MISTAKES.
ART IS KNOWING WHICH ONES TO KEEP."
—SCOTT ADAMS

Put a Smile on
Your Face

Next time you are unhappy, put a smile on your face.
Just smile as big as you can and feel it from your heart.
It's hard to smile and be unhappy at the same time.

It's even more interesting to pay attention to the part of
you that doesn't want to smile. Happiness, just like anything
else, needs to be worked on. We have to make an effort to feel
"at home" with happiness.

Be Healthy

You can't truly enjoy something unless your mind, health, and overall mood are on the same page. Health is one of the biggest factors in being happy. This is nothing new, but we can't hear it too many times.

- Water

- Rest

- Good nutrition

- Exercise

START FEELING BETTER!

Jesse

EXERCISE IS AN EXTREMELY IMPORTANT factor in finding and maintaining happiness. It may seem like it's obvious because we hear so often that exercise is good for us, but you'd be surprised at how many people don't connect it with being happy. Not only does exercise do wonders for your self-confidence and self-discipline, but it also naturally combats stress and promotes the release of endorphins in your body. Endorphins are compounds that act as painkillers and fever relievers, and that can make you feel a general sense of well-being.

A good first step to starting an exercise regimen is to build a realistic workout schedule for yourself, one you will be able to stick to. Draw or buy a calendar, and decide on three days that you can dedicate to exercising. Try to space them out evenly throughout the week. Now, for every week on your calendar, write in "Exercise Day" or something similar on each of the days that you chose. Whenever this day comes around, force yourself to get up and get in some sort of exercise. You can swim, lift weights, hike, or even just get in a game of soccer with some friends. After you complete the activity, cross it off your calendar. The simple act of crossing out the day you've completed should make you feel good about yourself. Without even knowing it, you will have boosted your self-esteem and you'll be a little healthier, too.

As you exercise more, you can get serious about your workouts and begin to add more days of exercise to the week. If you keep at it, you will be amazed at how good your body begins to feel, how your stress levels begin to lower, and how your mood will start to change for the better. Even at the two-week mark, you'll notice a change in how you feel. I promise you, it will be good. But be sure to talk to a healthcare specialist before beginning any workout regimen.

"THE SERENITY PRAYER"

God grant me

The serenity

To accept the things I cannot change

The courage

To change the things I can

And the wisdom

To know the difference.

Here's what this means:

- **Accept** the things I **cannot change**—
  that means other people, places, and things.

- **Courage** to change the **things I can**—
  that means myself

- And the **wisdom** to remember the difference—
  that means to keep in mind that other people
  and things **do not make me who I am**.

Clearing Toxins Through Breathing

id you know that when you exhale, toxins leave your body? Try this exercise:

Breathe . . .

Breathe . . .

Breathe . . .

Breathe with all your awareness. Breathe as **slow** as you can without getting tense.

Inhale . . .

Life

Oxygen

Tenderness

Calmness

Happiness

Exhale . . .

Tension

Rigidity

Negativity

Sadness

Do this several times. **You'll feel ENERGIZED.**

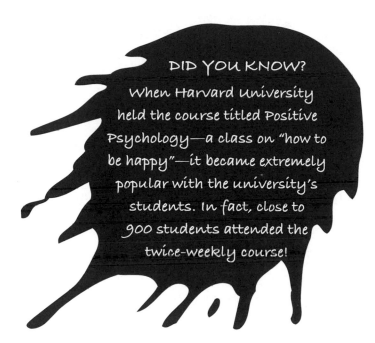

DID YOU KNOW?

When Harvard University held the course titled Positive Psychology—a class on "how to be happy"—it became extremely popular with the university's students. In fact, close to 900 students attended the twice-weekly course!

Keep a Positive Perspective

How we choose to look at things and what we choose to do about them has a lot to do with whether or not we live life from a happy place or from a negative, stressed-out place.

Happiness is a choice.

"HAPPINESS IS NOT A STATION YOU ARRIVE AT, BUT A MANNER OF TRAVELING."

—MARGARET LEE RUNBECK

I think it is safe to assume that happiness is the first thing on our "I want" list. We all want to be happy. After all, happiness is about liking what we do and doing what we like. Happiness is being comfortable with who we are. Happiness is a state where guilt and anger roll off our backs. It is the absence of fear, expectations, and judgments. When we are happy, we are at peace with ourselves and able to see what's right about things around us. It is being perfectly okay with now. There are no regrets about what happened in our past, and there are no fears or expectations about the future. Happiness is about being 100 percent in the present. Happiness is about being totally content with the way things are—right now.

Happiness is liking life exactly the way it is, right now. **EXACTLY the way it is right now.**

"FINISH EACH DAY
AND BE DONE WITH IT.
YOU HAVE DONE WHAT YOU COULD.
SOME BLUNDERS AND ABSURDITIES
NO DOUBT CREPT IN; FORGET
THEM AS SOON AS YOU CAN.
TOMORROW IS A NEW DAY;
BEGIN IT WELL AND SERENELY AND
WITH TOO HIGH A SPIRIT TO BE
ENCUMBERED WITH YOUR
OLD NONSENSE."

—RALPH WALDO EMERSON

Let Go of Wants

By letting go of negative things that have happened in the past, we are also letting go of the strong possibility that they will happen again. We are dropping all the negativity and "victim symptoms" that we attract by holding on to these things.

What we focus on is what we get. We need to begin **forgiving and forgetting**, learning from and letting go of, simplifying and organizing. We need to face each day expecting the best and doing our best not to hang out in the negativity from our past.

THE GOOD NEWS

Jesse

THE GOOD NEWS IS YOU don't have to try very hard to gain the capacity for happiness. We are all born with it. Realizing that you do have the power to get happy and that it is, in fact, your birthright should be comforting. There's nothing wrong with freebies. Once you understand that you have the ability to get happy, you must decide when you are ready to make the necessary commitments.

Start out by pinpointing the things that make you happy throughout the day, no matter how small they might seem. Pay attention to anything that makes you smile or just feels good, even if that feeling lasts for only a few seconds. Making sure that little things like these are a regular occurrence throughout your week will help you keep your momentum. For me, sometimes all it takes is renting a movie and ordering a pizza. It's nothing special, but it's something I know I can do whenever I'm feeling a little tired of life. For some people, it may be dancing naked in the mud by a river. This is fine too, as long as I don't have to watch.

Make "Happy Time"

Arrange some time for yourself to do something that will relax you and make you happy. Listen to music, watch a good movie, read a book, or maybe give yourself a pedicure. Here's how:

- **Soak your feet** in warm or comfortably hot water for as long as you like. Dry off your feet. Apply lotion. While applying, massage your feet. You don't need instructions for this. Just do what feels good to you. Don't forget to massage your toes.

Chicago Public Library
Greater Grand Crossing
4/21/2015   1:11:15 PM
-Patron Receipt-

EMS BORROWED:

tle: I don't know what I want /
em #: R0430262505
ue Date: 5/12/2015

-Please retain for your records-

HANEK

🌑 **Trim your toenails** and file them smooth. Apply polish if you desire. Let your feet do an air dance.

🌑 **Lay back with your feet propped up** and read a magazine or listen to music while your polish dries. If you didn't use polish, prop your feet up anyway and just relax. If time allows, follow your pedicure with a thirty-minute nap.

Now that is **happy time!**

When you stand up, take notice of how the earth feels under your feet. Remember, pedicures are not just for girls. In any case, if pedicures are not your thing, find the perfect activity that enables you to completely relax.

"All I Want Is a Smile"

Lia Gay

Recently, I had a terrible day at work. When I have bad days, my unhappiness usually bubbles up when I'm driving in my car. Dangerous, I know. My eyes were swollen from crying; my heart was beating fast with anxiety. **I felt like there was no way to get rid of that feeling.** And more than that, I thought there was no way to find happiness in that moment. I tried everything: breathing slow, listening to my favorite music, and even calling my mom. Still, the unhappiness and fear grew stronger. As I rounded the corner to my house, there was a man there, disheveled. He was holding a sign that read, "All I want is a smile."

Suddenly my heart stopped pounding. I thought to myself, *Here is a man with nothing, with every reason to be frowning, and there he was on the corner, smiling at strangers.* I smiled, of course, and the first feeling I felt was gratitude. Then, as I was pulling into my garage, I focused on being grateful that I had a home and a loving family. I realized that the gratitude and the smile I gave that man cured my unhappiness that day.

Lately, I've been trying to practice that when I feel unhappy. I try to think of even the smallest thing to feel grateful for, even if it's just that there is milk for my cereal in the morning. The other thing I do is try to smile—to myself, at someone else, even when I don't feel like smiling at all, because it reminds me of that man and his sign, **"All I want is a smile."**

Get Back to Basics

I t is the simplest things in life that give us the most
pleasure. **So, get back to the basics.** Reach out to
an old friend, take your dog for a long walk, spend some time
listening to your favorite music, enjoy a long relaxing bath,
or curl up with a good book. You get the idea. You'll find **joy**
in doing simple things.

"My Daily Pursuit of Happiness"

Chrissy Blumenthal

When I was younger, I always looked forward to holidays, birthdays, and extravagant events to bring me happiness. I would put so much emphasis on future occasions that I forgot how to live in the moment. I also made the mistake of believing that I would find happiness if I just met particular goals and reached life-changing milestones.

I thought I would be happy once we had a bigger apartment, when I got a boyfriend, when I lost ten pounds, when I had a hundred dollars in my savings account . . . my list was endless, and because my goals were such that achieving them all at once would never happen, something would always be missing. I set myself up to fail, and once I did, I would be anything but happy.

Eventually, I did meet a lot of those goals and milestones. I married a great man, had children, lost ten pounds (gained ten pounds), made a pretty decent salary, moved into a very nice house, and so on. Did those events make me happy? **Of course they did.** But did they make me permanently happy? **No.**

I don't believe there's any one thing that can bring permanent happiness. Not money. Not children. Not even love. Nothing can bring you constant and permanent happiness. We all have our ups and downs. We all have good and bad days. And we all experience happy and sad times. There's no doubt that money, marriage, children, and good health bring a lot of people plenty of happiness, but are they eternally happy? Probably not, because, as with so many good things in life, this type of happiness can't last forever.

Consequently, instead of looking to future events to bring me happiness, and instead of searching for perpetual happiness, I have been practicing "my daily pursuit of happiness." And I think I've finally succeeded. I can finally say, "I'm happy every day." It's not so hard to find something that brings you a little bit of joy or a smile to your face, every single day.

Here are just a few things I have found that bring me daily happiness:

A great meal when I am "starved"

A smile from a hot guy

A day with no responsibilities

Something new or really cool to wear

A long talk on the phone with an old friend

My hair drying perfectly

A great song on the radio

Great music to sing with

A warm, relaxing bubble bath

A great movie at home with snacks

No dirty clothes in my room

A good sale

A walk on the beach

A clean room

A good television show on a night with no homework

A clean bill of health, feeling good, being well rested

The weekend!

READER/CUSTOMER CARE SURVEY

We care about your opinions! Please take a moment to fill out our online Reader Survey at
http://survey.hcibooks.com. As a **"THANK YOU"** you will receive a **VALUABLE INSTANT COUPON** towards future
book purchases as well as a **SPECIAL GIFT** available only online! Or, you may mail this card back to us.

First Name _____ MI. _____ Last Name _____

Address _____

State _____ Zip _____ Email _____ City _____

1. Gender
☐ Female ☐ Male

2. Age
☐ 8 or younger
☐ 9-12   ☐ 13-16
☐ 17-20   ☐ 21-30
☐ 31+

**3. Did you receive
this book as a gift?**
☐ Yes   ☐ No

**4. Annual
Household Income**
☐ under $25,000
☐ $25,000 - $34,999
☐ $35,000 - $49,999
☐ $50,000 - $74,999
☐ over $75,000

**5. What are the
ages of the children
living in your house?**
☐ 0 - 14   ☐ 15+

6. Marital Status
☐ Single
☐ Married
☐ Divorced
☐ Widowed

Comments _____
_____
_____
_____
_____
_____

BUSINESS REPLY MAIL

FIRST-CLASS MAIL   PERMIT NO 45   DEERFIELD BEACH, FL

POSTAGE WILL BE PAID BY ADDRESSEE

Health Communications, Inc.
3201 SW 15th Street
Deerfield Beach FL 33442-9875

"Remember to Remember"

Lia Gay

The other day, someone told me that when you are unhappy, it's hard to remember that you can be happy again. When we are happy, we feel like we did something to **deserve** that happiness. So in turn, when we are unhappy, we have a tendency to **beat ourselves up** thinking that we must have done something to deserve that too. The truth is that happiness is not about deserving, and so in turn, neither is unhappiness. The happiest times in my life are the times where I can find something in myself to feel proud of, to feel good about. The happiest times are the times when I find it inside, not from the outside world.

"Get Organized"

Hana Szabo

There are times when nothing makes me smile, when everything just seems to fall apart right before my eyes. When life gets complicated, sometimes the only thing that can cheer me up is a good deep cleaning. Cleaning? I know, not fun! But when I'm done, and I look around and everything is in its place, I feel centered. I feel on top of things. I feel organized. I sit in my immaculate room, and I have a sense of clarity. Not to mention waking up in a room that's clean gives an exciting, fresh start to my day.

The Gratitude Attitude

Gratitude is all about the attitude. If you are grateful, it is a pleasure to do things for you and to be your friend. Think about how good you feel in the presence of someone who is thankful for your friendship, who genuinely appreciates you. Think about how nice it is to be with people who are, for the most part, happy with the way life treats them. When things don't work out, they look at what they might have done to get a better result. They don't blame others for their predicament.

"Every Day Something New"

Cody Demory

Every day I try to go out and teach myself something new. In my case, it's mostly on a skateboard. When I struggle to learn a certain trick, I try over and over until I know I can land it every time. When I finally have that trick on lock, I get overwhelmed with this euphoric state of happiness. It only lasts a second, but after that I know that I've taught myself something new and that's all that matters. That's what makes me the happiest.

"I'VE BEEN GIVEN"

Kristen Foster

I've been given shoulders to cry on,
And a brain to help me think.
I've been given arms to welcome friends,
And legs to get around,
A conscience to show me what is right,
And feet to connect to the ground.

I've been given a nose to smell changes,
And the good that they can cause,
A pair of eyes to see good friends,
As I overlook their flaws.

I've been given guts to stand up,
And faith to look above
I've been given hands to mold the world,
And a heart to show it love.

Say Thank You!

Write a letter to someone you haven't properly thanked for something he or she has done! Pay attention to how good it feels. Pay attention to the pleasure you get thinking about the day the letter is received, the smile it will merit, and who you think the recipient will show it to first. **Gratitude goes a long way.**

"THE ONLY GUARANTEE
THAT HUMAN INTELLIGENCE
WILL BE USED PROPERLY IS TO
ENSURE THAT IT IS GUIDED
BY A GOOD HEART."
—THE DALAI LAMA

Give in Return

lbert Einstein reflected on the purpose of man's existence when he said:

"Strange is our situation here upon earth. Each of us comes for a short visit, not knowing why, yet sometimes seeming to a divine purpose. From the standpoint of daily life, however, there is one thing we do know: that we are here for the sake of others . . . for the countless unknown souls with whose fate we are connected by a bond of sympathy. Many times a day, I realize how much my outer and inner life is built upon the labors of people, both living and dead, and how earnestly I must exert myself in order to give in **return as much** as I have received."

There is more happiness
In giving than in receiving.

BEFORE YOU BEGIN THIS JOURNEY
TOWARD BEING HAPPY,
IT IS VERY IMPORTANT THAT YOU KNOW
EXACTLY
WHERE YOU
WANT TO GO.

Discipline Your Emotions

Most of us give **our emotions so much power that we end up enslaved to them.** We forget that we choose how we react to things. We aren't aware that there are things we can do to discipline our feelings so we aren't always reacting to things **uncontrollably**. We have to remember that **we are responsible** for how we feel and how our life unfolds, and it is up to us to make sure things stay in a **positive** place.

"HAPPINESS COMES WHEN
YOUR WORK AND WORDS ARE OF
BENEFIT TO YOURSELF
AND OTHERS."

—BUDDHA

Give Someone a Hand

Help someone out. The **simple act** of helping **others** helps us feel good. Pick up groceries for an aging neighbor, volunteer at your local hospital, or read a book to someone with failing eyesight. If you are unsure of how to help out in your community, call your nearest volunteer center.

THE POWER OF LAUGHTER

Jesse

STRESS, ANXIETY, AND DEPRESSION WILL never stand a chance against an individual who can disarm their power with laughter. If you've ever driven anywhere in a big city, you have a good idea of how often humans are being bombarded by scenarios that can manifest in our bodies as negative feelings. When I'm driving around in Los Angeles, I feel like something is wrong if I don't get cut off at least ten times while on the road.

Instead of flashing the local species of bird, I'll usually smile and say, "Thank you very much! You're a wonderful driver!" This allows me to laugh at the situation instead of letting it ruin my mood. It may be a small moment, but every little bit helps. When you find yourself laughing at a moment that should induce anger and stress, you'll notice that you gain a whole new perspective on what's going on. Not only will you benefit immediately, you will start to spot negative situations before they can get to you. Just like anything else (except my attempts at skiing), practice makes perfect. The more you laugh at frustrating moments, the easier it will become.

Have a Light Heart

The more difficult the challenges, the more horrible the circumstances, the more stressful the situation, the more you must learn to laugh. The ability to be lighthearted in situations that would otherwise create stress is the key.

Here are some ingredients for creating happiness in your life:

No more blaming the outside.

No more blaming your friends and family.

No more blaming yourself.

No more blaming, period!

Laugh, smile, help!

"IT IS NOT LENGTH OF LIFE,
BUT DEPTH OF LIFE."
—RALPH WALDO EMERSON

You Are Stronger Than You Think

When we are able to recognize our hurts as our teachers and we aren't afraid to feel some pain, we are able to take the past and learn great things from it. You are much stronger than you think. It takes more strength to push things away and ignore them than it does to relax, breathe, and experience them.

When we attempt to not feel, the amount of energy that is consumed is far more than if we simply allow things to happen organically. By allowing and accepting life just as it is, we can learn so much. We begin to be more flexible. We have more energy and vitality. When things are able to flow freely on the inside, our outside follows suit. **All this leaves us a little bit wiser** and **a lot happier**.

"ONE JOY SHATTERS A
HUNDRED GRIEFS."

—CHINESE PROVERB

Keep the Power

When we worry too much about what other people think of us or we want to be perceived in a certain way, we tend to give away our power. We don't want to say the wrong thing or do the wrong thing because we are invested in other people seeing us in a certain way—a way that is different from our real selves.

When we do something different from what we feel, or we say something we don't really mean, we have given our power to the person we are trying to impress. What they think of us means more to us than how we make someone else feel or, more important, how we make ourselves feel. We sell ourselves short. **We give away our power**.

The irony in this is that almost 100% of the time the very people we are trying to impress by not being real would like us far better if we stood up for ourselves or if we just put ourselves out there and said:

"LIKE ME OR NOT, HERE I AM!"

JESSE'S ROOM

Jesse

ONE NIGHT I ENDED UP ADDING TWO HOLES to my door when it really didn't need any at all, just because I let my anger and frustration get the best of me. Very stupid. It hurt, and I had to pay to fix it. Not only that, I wasn't exactly proud when I had to explain to my friends why my door now provided my room with more ventilation.

Emotions exist as a sort of navigation device for our bodies. They motivate us to head toward the things that we feel good about and help us to steer clear of things that might be bad for us. As with any other device, malfunctions can occur. Our emotions can cause us to do some brash and ridiculous things in the moment without the presence of rational thoughts. It is a bit of a confusing situation because logical thoughts can help us control our emotions, but it is difficult, and sometimes impossible, to think logically when you're in an emotional state. Then what are you supposed to do? I've already ruled out punching solid objects, as it doesn't seem to help very much. Try learning to use your thoughts to help you control your negative emotions before they have a chance to control you. Instead of immediately acting out in a burst of sadness or anger, use rational thought to extinguish the flame. Am I going to feel this way forever? Definitely not. So why should I let this feeling take control of me? I shouldn't.

The more you practice taking control over your negative emotions, the more you will notice that you are experiencing them less often and with less intensity.

Think Differently

don't know if you've noticed this, but we don't exactly live in a warm and fuzzy world, which is the opposite of what I used to think. I believed people would be happy if a friend got an A on a test for which he studied hard.

I thought if I looked pretty, it would evoke a positive reaction from my friends. I thought that if I woke up in a good mood, it would carry throughout the day. Then I'd get to school, and it would seem like everyone was out to get me.

These are the days when you really need to have tough skin.

Believe me when I say I know how cruel the world can be and how important it is to be tough.

You can't change the world. No matter how much you want to, it isn't going to happen. You can, however, change the way you react to it. It's really important to remember who you are and make a point to never forget it. The more you can define yourself, the less others can do it for you.

If you know you are a kind person, and you stick by that, no one will be able to convince you otherwise. Let them say whatever they want.

You know who you are.

The next thing to learn is how to say no when something doesn't work for you and to set your boundaries in such a clear way that you don't have a problem sticking to them. In doing so, you will figure out what you're willing to do and what you are not. This is what you believe in and this is what you don't believe in. Promise yourself that no matter what, you won't go outside of those boundaries. These are all parts of getting strong.

Every time you stand up for what you believe in or stay true to the goals you have set for yourself, you strengthen those muscles. **You become stronger.** With this strength, you gain the faith necessary to really understand that you can have what you want.

Keep your eye on the prize!

RESOLUTIONS

Jesse

RESOLUTIONS HAVE SOMEHOW BECOME MARKED as something that we only need to make once a year. One reason for this may be that it makes it much easier for us to commit to something if we're able to wait all year to actually do anything about it. Procrastination is such an easy path to take because it provides the built-in relief of not having to do any work right away. But the night before the deadline, you always find yourself freaking out. That sounds a lot like every Sunday night of my high-school career.

Resolutions should instead be viewed as something we can make whenever we feel that a change is necessary.

As soon as you realize that you aren't happy, that is the best time to start working toward happiness—not at the end of the year. Start making resolutions to better your life as soon as you feel the urge. The more you complete, the more your confidence in yourself will build to help with your bigger resolutions.

"Picking Up the Pieces"

Emily Starr

I struggled for weeks, desperately trying to be the legs on which our tottering relationship could balance. Eventually, everything toppled over, and all I could do was just stand there, staring, overcome with shock and anguish, yet too exhausted to pick up the pieces.

I could have blamed it on him. He had betrayed my trust one too many times. He was too lazy and immature. Or I could have blamed it on myself. I was too committed and overprotective.

But the more I thought about it, the more I realized that our relationship was strangely similar to the game where you stack narrow blocks of wood on top of one another in rows of three. Everything started out solid and sturdy, but as the months progressed, pieces of the whole were withdrawn until the shaky structure crumbled to the ground in a heap of hurt feelings, angry tears, and painful memories.

The day "us" ended haunted my mind for weeks. I thought I could read every look on his face, but that day he wore an expression completely unfamiliar to me. I asked him what was wrong, but deep inside I knew what he was going to say. His eyes pleaded with mine, and I remember slowly taking off the jacket he had lent me earlier that day. I pressed it to my cheek, breathed in the familiar scent, and handed it to him while tears began to flood my eyes.

He brushed one aside with his finger and walked away without a single word. I remember looking down at my outcast arms that hung in the air, empty and bare without a soul to reach out to. There weren't any strong arms to hold me, and there wasn't a soothing voice to subdue the pain.

Alexander Graham Bell was believed to have said, "When one door closes, another opens; but we often look so long and so regretfully upon the closed door that we do not see the ones which open for us." I was staring at the door that had been slammed in my face. I stood looking through the keyhole at him living his own life. His life no longer involved me.

I banged on the door; I kicked and screamed till I was dizzy, but all I could do was stand outside, looking in.

One day I began to realize that in the midst of all my pain, I had neglected everything that was once important to me. I found myself standing there friendless, my family completely shoved away, and several months of my youth wasted on a foolish, teenage boy.

A wave of relaxation washed over me, and I knew then and there that I was going to be my own person and rely on no one but myself for my happiness. I was going to forgive myself for past mistakes and start over.

That day, I would begin to live my own life, no matter who decided to slam the door in my face. Relationships are always collapsing, but **only the strong can pick up the pieces** and rebuild their lives using their experiences as footholds the next time around.

"The Journey"

Zan Gaudisio

always thought that my happiness would come as a natural byproduct of the milestones I would achieve in life. My best friend shared this belief, and we served as each other's support systems while we worked our way, milestone by milestone, to perfect happiness.

She had just married the man of her dreams when she was diagnosed. Leukemia was clearly not in our mapped-out plan for happiness. We had grown up together, two smart, funny, attractive, overachieving girls of baby boomer parents. How could we not achieve all the goals we had in place for a happy life?

As we fought her disease, through bone marrow transplants, platelet infusions, sterile environments, nausea, weakness, and baldness, I watched happiness take another route. Through it all, my friend wanted to work, play, give, and learn more than ever. Her husband would say to me, "Doesn't she realize how much money I make? She doesn't have to do anything." But the truth is, she did.

She had to live, and so did I.

This moment of clarity was conscious and deliberate and came from watching her. I had to sift this new information through my brain to make sense of it. Her change was organic and natural. She was happy from doing things that would make her happy in the moment. She took piano lessons, not because of the Mozart concerto she would one day master, but because she liked to. It was something she always wanted to do and it made her happy. We've heard that true happiness is found in the moment and that joy is in the journey. I was beginning to learn that by watching my friend put aside our well-laid plans for happiness and just be happy.

She died in her home surrounded by her family and friends and her handmade awards from children at the City of Hope, to whom she had brought a great deal of happiness. Her last days were spent doing the things she wanted to do and contributing to the happiness of others because that made her happy. Her moments of gentleness and kindness to another would perpetuate more kindness and that would live on longer than she would. She died happy, knowing that she had contributed to making the world a little bit better just because she had passed through.

Today, I still have goals and plans, but I don't forget to enjoy where I am at the moment. I suck as much joy out of life as I can. When possible, I contribute and give to the happiness of others because I know its contagious nature. I now know that even the **smallest gesture of kindness** will continue to live long after I do.

What Causes Sadness?

There are certain conditions that make it very difficult to maintain a happy state. **Happiness** requires a certain amount of **energy**, and when we are run down, overtired, or not well nourished, it is close to impossible to stay on top of the things that life throws our way.

SADNESS can be looked at as the absence of happiness. For whatever reason, we just aren't happy. We often think it takes something that happens to make us sad, but more often than not, sadness may be due to something that isn't happening, something we need.

Here are some things that can cause sadness:

- 🦠 Not getting enough sleep

- 🦠 Too much junk food and not enough good nutrition

- 🦠 Loneliness; we need to be with other people. It's
  nice to have alone time, but we need to be sure
  we don't spend too much time by ourselves.

- 🦠 Not communicating. If we are upset, angry, or hurt,
  we should talk to someone. More often than not,
  giving words to our feelings allows us to put
  them in perspective.

If we didn't get sad sometimes, how could we be happy?
Really? Life is about opposites . . . things going right and things
going wrong. But if sadness becomes your home base and
there is no apparent reason, then this is worth looking into.
Who wants to be sad all the time and not even know why?

I don't believe there are easy answers to sadness, depression, or anxiety, and there are no easy fixes either. If you feel sad, depressed, or anxious, it is advisable to seek professional help. But also please remember that *you* are the one with most of the answers, even though plenty of people will be happy to give you theirs. Stay focused on healing, improving, and learning throughout this entire experience. Don't give yourself over to anyone but a higher power, pray a lot, and listen for the soft and kind voice giving you answers.

"WHEN YOU FEEL SAD, WRITE!
WRITE IT ALL OUT, GET IT ON PAPER,
FOR MORE THAN ONE REASON:
IT'S THERAPEUTIC,
IT GETS THE EMOTIONS OUT
IN A SAFE WAY, BUT ALSO
WHEN YOU'RE OVER WHATEVER IS
MAKING YOU SAD, IT'LL BE COOL
TO READ IT AND LAUGH
ABOUT IT LATER."

—HANA SZABO

Take Your Power Back

We have given our power away, so how do we get it back?

- By owning ourselves and **everything** about us.

- By taking **responsibility** for ourselves and our actions.

- By knowing that in any given moment we can **choose to be happy** no matter what is happening.

Be Honest, Be Patient, Be Real

How often have you had to listen to friends complain endlessly and blame other people for a situation you watched them create for themselves?

Facing up to the fact that we are in a really bad situation because of the choices we have made is not an easy thing to do. Regardless, it is the first step in changing for the better. The minute we own our actions, take responsibility for our plights, and admit when we have made mistakes, we are free to change. Until then, we use all our energy trying to defend ourselves against the truth. It can be exhausting. When we finally **let go** of our pride and **stop lying** to others and ourselves, it is such a relief that we can't even believe we were so scared. Every time we decide to tell the truth instead of lying, we free up so much **energy** that we will be able to reach our goals in half the time.

Learn the Difference Between the Cheap Thrills and the Real Thing

There are many ways to seek a cheap thrill—to laugh and smile and have all of your problems go away for a little while. Drinking, drugs, sex, new clothes—these are some of the things people reach for to quiet their sadness or emptiness. Things that make you "feel better" only for the moment are cheap thrills. A cheap thrill works for a little while, but once you realize that setting a goal and working hard to achieve it brings a smile that signals true happiness, you won't need cheap thrills. A "quick fix" can only last so long. But something you work hard for that made you grow as a person and made you push through tough obstacles gives you the kind of happiness that doesn't go away. You will also realize that you have the strength to make other things happen. Once you understand this, there is **no limit** to the **happiness you can have**.

INSTANT GRATIFICATION

Jesse

THE NEED FOR INSTANT GRATIFICATION is a tricky one. It's the little devil that sits on your shoulder, whispering in your ear to do whatever it take to make you feel better as soon as possible.

The tricky part is that he sometimes sounds reasonable, like he knows what he's talking about, but deep down we know he's a moron.

I recently had a hard time doing battle with my need for instant gratification, or more specifically my "need" for an Xbox 360. I had wanted one ever since they came out, but for one reason or another, I could never get one. Come to think of it, the only reason was that my wallet had a constant shortage of presidential occupants. My roommate at the time had received one as a gift for Christmas, and once I had been able to try it out, I was in the living room every morning playing it like my life depended on it.

He eventually moved out, and I was left to continue on without the little white box of joy (so what, I'm a dork). I had given up the idea of ever getting one within the next decade, until one day I found myself with four hundred dollars in cash from a recent job. You can probably assume what I immediately wanted to spend it on. I looked at my phone and noticed that it was 8:15 PM. The video game store closed at 9:00 PM, and my girlfriend wanted to get some dinner. Of course, the little instant gratification devil was telling me that I had to have the Xbox that night. After a pointless attempt at convincing my girlfriend that dinner was overrated, I hurried her into my car and sped to the restaurant. I tried my best to order and finish my food as fast as humanly possible and about halfway through, I realized that there was no way to make it to the store in time.

My girlfriend tried to make me feel better by saying that we could go the next morning to get it. It wasn't any consolation to me because I didn't want it the next day. I wanted it right away. After a while, I began to realize how ridiculous I was acting and started to put things into perspective.

It occurred to me that my bank account had a balance of about, oh, say, nine dollars and seventy-five cents, and that I couldn't afford to be blowing four hundred bucks on a machine wrapped in white plastic, even if it was really nice white plastic. I realized that I would be surviving on flour and water for the next few weeks if I decided to get the Xbox. In the end, I realized that eating was probably a little more important than destroying virtual mutants, and I decided to hold off on the purchase. My decision made me feel really good about myself, and let me tell you, food tasted even better that month.

Understanding Depression & Getting Help

The *Encarta World English Dictionary* defines depression as:

1. A state of unhappiness and hopelessness

2. A psychiatric disorder showing symptoms such as persistent feelings of hopelessness, dejection, poor concentration, lack of energy, inability to sleep, and, sometimes, suicidal tendencies

There are some situations where happiness is not as simple as a decision or a choice. When the body is chemically imbalanced, the result can be depression. When this happens, it is important to speak with your parents, a school counselor, a doctor, and/or other health professionals.

A good diet and regular exercise, along with balancing work and play, social time, and alone time, will be helpful if you are feeling depressed. They are, of course, helpful for avoiding it as well.

Depression is not something you can just "get over." Recognize the signs of depression, and if they apply to you, seek professional help. These are some of the signs of depression:

- Feeling **empty** and **numb**

- Feeling **hopeless** (like there's nothing to look forward to)

- Feeling **guilty** or **worthless**

- Feeling **lonely** and **unloved**

- Feeling **irritated** and **annoyed** a lot (at every little thing)

- Feeling like things are **not fun** anymore

- Having **trouble** keeping your mind on school and work

- Having **less energy** and feeling tired all the time

- **Sleeping** too much or not enough

- **Not eating** enough or weighing enough

- Thinking about **death** or **suicide**

- Spending **less time with friends** and **more time alone**

- **Crying** a lot, often for no reason

- Feeling **restless** (being unable to sit or relax)

If you have a few of these symptoms, your sadness may have escalated to depression, and it is very important that you seek help. If you have sadness that simply won't go away, it is depression. **It is easier to recover from a deep, dark place with help from others.** There is **always** somebody to talk to: a friend, your parents, a school counselor, your doctor, a mental-health professional, a hotline, and so on.

"I VIEW HAPPINESS AS DEEPER
THAN A MOMENTARY GOOD MOOD—
AS AN ENDURING SENSE
OF POSITIVE WELL-BEING, AN
ONGOING PERCEPTION THAT LIFE
IS FULFILLING, MEANINGFUL,
AND PLEASANT."

—DAVID MEYERS

DID YOU KNOW?

Attitude has a lot to do with how happy you are; if you wake up in a bad mood, you're not even giving happiness a chance to sneak in. Your attitude toward your day, especially when you first wake up, has a lot to do with how much happiness you'll be letting in that day. Just be aware, having a negative attitude is a happiness blocker!

Some Questions for You to Ask Yourself

When you're trying to figure out what you're all about, it helps to ask yourself some questions. Here are some for you to start with. Write your answers in a journal. In a few weeks, answer the questions again, and see how your answers differ, if at all. This will help you figure out what you really want and need from life.

What really makes you **happy**?

How do **you** define happiness?

What **things** or **people** in your life make you happy?

What do your **parents** think makes you happy?

Is your **opinion** different from theirs?

What do you **really** want?

Define "**want.**"

What **kinds** of people do you want in your life?

What do your parents **think** you want?

Is your **opinion** different from theirs?

What do other **people** want?

What would you **like** to do?

Who or what would you like to **love**?

What do you **hope** for?

What do you **want**?

Who makes you **smile**?

What did you **want** when you were younger?

How is that **different** from what you want now?

Do you need **certain** things to make you happy?

What are they?

Do you **think** about being happy often?

Do you **believe** happiness is your birthright?

What does this **mean** to you?

Do you believe being happy is your **duty**?

What does this mean to **you**?

What's the one **place, person, and situation** that fuels you with happiness?

Do you believe you can **choose** to be happy?

How much does the past **affect** your present happiness?

What about your past makes you feel ashamed or angry?

What's usually
the first thing
you think
about when
you wake up in
the morning?

LET GO OF OLD
BAGGAGE SO YOU HAVE
AN EMPTY SUITCASE
READY TO BE FILLED WITH
NEW, EXCITING STUFF.
THE MORE YOU LET GO
OF, THE MORE
ROOM YOU HAVE.

Does that **affect**
the rest of your
day?

Another angle of happiness is doing **good deeds for others**.
List a couple of scenarios when you did something for
someone else and you felt great about it.

What makes **people** around you happy?

What makes your **best friend** happy?

What makes your **parents** happy?

What makes
your little
brother or
sister happy?

Do you see how

different

everyone's

happiness is?

ONCE YOU'RE
AWARE OF EVERYONE'S
HAPPINESS, YOU'LL BE
MORE AWARE OF
YOUR OWN.
NOT EVERYONE
IS THE SAME.

What do you **do** when you're unhappy?

What is in the way of you and your **perfect** happiness?

Make a list of everything that is standing in the way of you and your happiness? (LEAVE NOTHING OFF THE LIST.) When your list is complete, begin planning what you will do to cross everything off. (AND OF COURSE HAVE A MARKER HANDY FOR CROSSING THINGS OFF.)

Isn't it interesting how people tend to think about their unhappiness more than happiness? Which one are you more aware of? How happy or unhappy are you?

_____

_____

_____

_____

_____

_____

_____

_____

_____

_____

Happiness Is a Choice

Happiness is a choice; you can decide if you want to be happy every single day for the rest of your life. I know this sounds crazy, but in reality, you are in full control of your happiness. Happiness in this case does not mean a new car or concert tickets; it can be a minute thing that will always bring you your daily happiness.

I personally am the happiest when I see a smile on the face of someone I love—especially if I am the one who put the smile there. This doesn't take much effort, but the outcome is enormous!

Just for today, when you leave your home and go into the world, walk with your head held high, smile at strangers passing by, stay in your "I'm having a great day zone," and see if that **changes your mood** and your day overall.

No two people are alike, so it would be impossible to come up with one universal thing that makes everyone happy. Sure, there are things like money, jewelry, and cars that would make many people happy, but that's not the kind of happiness I'm speaking of. I don't mean the "I just got a brand new ride and I'm thrilled, but really none of my problems went away so I'm just temporarily smiling until my problems dawn on me again" kind of happiness. I mean little things—**it's all about the little things**. Things like getting chores done, making sure you spend time with your brothers and sisters, finishing your homework early, and making sure your room is clean. **How can you not feel amazing when your life is so on track?**

ACKNOWLEDGMENTS

I am so grateful to have the opportunity to acknowledge and thank the people who helped get this book from our hearts into your hands. From concept to delivery, this has been a huge undertaking that tested everyone's commitment and devotion to its message.

I want to thank the staff at HCI for their patience and assistance. Thank you, Peter. I believe the good guys win, but *when* isn't always in our control. Keep doing the right thing.

I also want to thank all of the teens who helped us. Some of them would drop whatever they were doing to come over and help us review covers. My friends Changa and Brie were always happy to review material and do interviews. I love you guys. Zach and friends, thanks for helping so much at such a crucial time.

Hanna, you are my lifeline—with a generous heart, a smile (usually), and a great attitude. You will always be my friend, my sister, and my precious daughter. Thanks for everything. You brought smiles for me and that's a big thing when you have been working on a book for so long. I will never forget what you've done for me. I also want to thank Brian Mayfield, whose support was given in so many different ways.

Thanks to Jack, Ricky, Taylor, Taycora, Jayde, Zach, Tana, Mary, Bobby, Daddy Fred and Toni, Taylor Girl, Christopher, Oran, Kyle, Inga, Travis, and Riley. You are my family and that is at the top of the list of what makes me happy. Tammy, Ashlee, and Trevor—your positive attitude and all your help has been an inspiration. I want to give a big thanks to all the guys at Shutters who made the editing process comfortable and doable. A special thanks to Danielle, Mike, Scott, George, et al.

A big thank-you to Alexander Witt for being an inspiration to me and an example to adhere to. Gracie, David and Sonia, you were here when it wasn't easy, and I can't express my gratitude in words. Zan and Jake, you are special people. Thanks for all.

—Kimberly Kirberger